Easy Learning

Mental maths practice

Age 5-7

My name is _____.

I am _____ years old.

I go to _____ School.

My birthday is _____.

Peter Clarke

How to use this book

- Find a quiet, comfortable place to work, away from other distractions.

- Ask your child what maths topic they are doing at school, and choose an appropriate topic.

- Tackle one topic at a time.

- Help with reading the instructions where necessary, and ensure that your child understands what they are required to do.

- Help and encourage your child to check their own answers as they complete each activity.

- Discuss with your child what they have learnt.

- Let your child return to their favourite pages once they have been completed, to play the games and talk about the activities.

- Reward your child with plenty of praise and encouragement.

Special features

- Yellow boxes: Introduce and outline the key maths ideas.

- Example boxes: Show how to do the activity.

- Yellow shaded boxes: Offer advice to parents on how to consolidate your child's understanding.

- Games: Some of the topics include a game, which reinforces the topic. Some of these games require a spinner. This is easily made using a pencil, a paperclip and the circle printed on each games page. Gently flick the paperclip with your finger to make it spin.

Published by Collins
An imprint of HarperCollins*Publishers*
77–85 Fulham Palace Road
Hammersmith
London
W6 8JB

Browse the complete Collins catalogue at
www.collins.co.uk

© HarperCollins*Publishers* Limited 2012

10 9 8 7 6 5 4 3 2

ISBN 978-0-00-750504-3

The author asserts his moral right to be identified as the author of this work.

British Library Cataloguing in Publication Data

A Catalogue record for this publication is available from the British Library

The author wishes to thank Brian Molyneaux for his valuable contribution to this publication.

Written by Peter Clarke
Page design by G Brasnett, Cambridge
Illustrated by Kathy Baxendale, Rachel Annie Bridgen and Graham Smith
Cover design by Linda Miles, Lodestone Publishing Ltd
Cover illustration by Kathy Baxendale
Commissioned by Tammy Poggo
Project managed by Chantal Peacock
Production by Rebecca Evans
Printed and bound by Printing Express, Hong Kong

MIX
Paper from
responsible sources
FSC™ C007454

FSC™ is a non-profit international organisation established to promote the responsible management of the world's forests. Products carrying the FSC label are independently certified to assure consumers that they come from forests that are managed to meet the social, economic and ecological needs of present and future generations, and other controlled sources.

Find out more about HarperCollins and the environment at
www.harpercollins.co.uk/green

Contents

Numbers 1

Q1 Write the missing numbers.

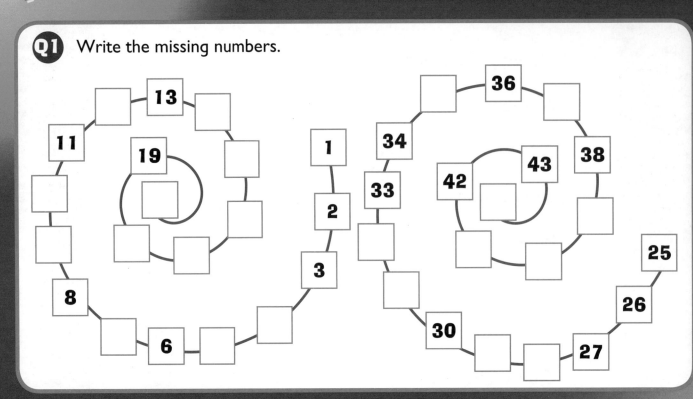

Q2 Put each set of numbers in order, smallest first.

4	10	2	6	9	8

5	12	17	7	1	11

25	36	3	30	41	18

Look at all the numbers in the blue boxes. Write these numbers in order, smallest first.

Game: Larger card wins

You need: pack of playing cards with the Jacks, Queens and Kings removed

- Shuffle the cards and deal them out so that each player has the same number of cards.
- Each player:
  - places their cards face down in a pile
  - turns over the top card from their pile.
- The player with the larger number is the winner of that round and takes both cards, putting them to one side.
- The game continues in this way.
- The winner is the player with more cards once each player has revealed all their cards.

Variation

- Play 'Smaller card wins'. The player with the smaller number is the winner of that round.

Q3 Write the missing numbers.

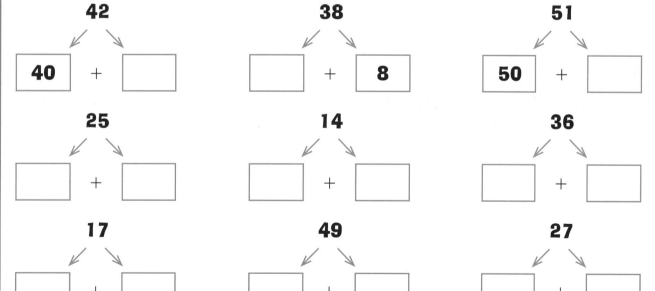

42
40 + ☐

38
☐ + 8

51
50 + ☐

25
☐ + ☐

14
☐ + ☐

36
☐ + ☐

17
☐ + ☐

49
☐ + ☐

27
☐ + ☐

In order to calculate with numbers, it is important that your child is able to count, recognise, read, write, compare and order numbers to 20 then 100. They also need to have a secure understanding of place value, i.e. 46 = 40 + 6.

Addition 1

A number line helps with addition. We can use it to **count on** from the larger number.

3 + 4 = 7

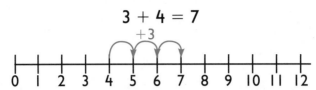

Q1 Write the missing numbers.

3 + 1 = ☐   6 + 2 = ☐   10 + 0 = ☐

2 + 5 = ☐   3 + 3 = ☐   4 + 4 = ☐

5 + 5 = ☐   4 + 2 = ☐   6 + 3 = ☐

7 + 2 = ☐   9 + 1 = ☐   2 + 8 = ☐

4 + ☐ = 7   2 + ☐ = 4   ☐ + 5 = 8

☐ + 1 = 9   5 + ☐ = 9   ☐ + 3 = 5

Q2 Write the missing numbers.

2 + 3 + 1 = ☐   2 + 4 + 3 = ☐   3 + ☐ + 2 = 9

4 + 2 + 2 = ☐   5 + 1 + 2 = ☐   ☐ + 1 + 7 = 10

1 + 2 + 5 = ☐   2 + 2 + 3 + 4 = ☐   6 + 2 + ☐ = 11

4 + 1 + 5 = ☐   3 + 2 + 1 + 1 = ☐   5 + ☐ + 4 = 12

Game: Add the dice

You need: two 1 – 6 dice, 20 counters

- Before you start, decide who will have which wing of the butterfly.
- Take turns to:
  - roll both dice
  - add the two numbers together
  - put a counter on that answer on your wing of the butterfly.
- If the answer is already covered on your wing, miss that go.
- The winner is the first player to cover 6 of the numbers on their wing.

Q3 Write pairs of numbers that total 10 and 20.

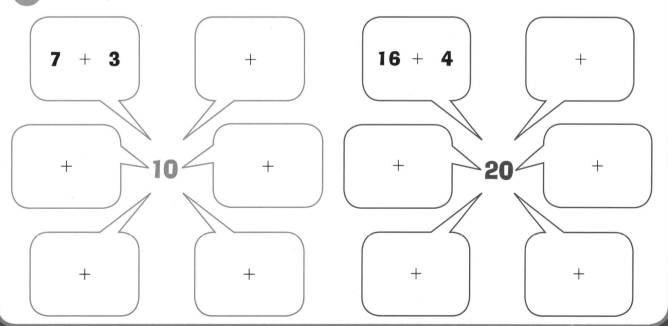

7 + 3   ☐ + ☐   16 + 4   ☐ + ☐

☐ + ☐   **10**   ☐ + ☐   ☐ + ☐   **20**   ☐ + ☐

☐ + ☐   ☐ + ☐   ☐ + ☐   ☐ + ☐

Subtraction 1

We can think of subtraction as **taking away**.

You can **count back** from the larger number along a number line to help you take away.

$$6 - 2 = 4$$

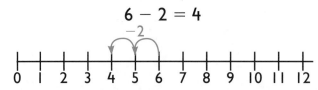

Q1 Answer these.

$3 - 1 = \boxed{}$ $6 - 2 = \boxed{}$ $4 - 3 = \boxed{}$

$7 - 2 = \boxed{}$ $5 - 2 = \boxed{}$ $2 - 2 = \boxed{}$

$8 - 5 = \boxed{}$ $10 - 8 = \boxed{}$ $6 - 3 = \boxed{}$

$7 - 4 = \boxed{}$ $9 - 3 = \boxed{}$ $5 - 4 = \boxed{}$

We can also think of subtraction as **finding the difference** between two numbers.

You can **count on** from the smaller number along a number line to help you take away.

$$6 - 2 = 4$$

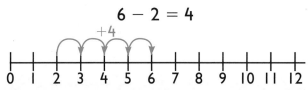

Q2 Answer these.

$5 - 3 = \boxed{}$ $4 - 1 = \boxed{}$ $7 - 3 = \boxed{}$

$10 - 5 = \boxed{}$ $6 - 4 = \boxed{}$ $8 - 7 = \boxed{}$

$9 - 6 = \boxed{}$ $3 - 2 = \boxed{}$ $10 - 7 = \boxed{}$

$8 - 3 = \boxed{}$ $4 - 2 = \boxed{}$ $9 - 2 = \boxed{}$

Game: Difference dice

You need: two 1 – 6 dice, 20 counters

- Before you start, decide who will have which wing of the ladybird.
- Take turns to:
  - roll both dice
  - find the difference between the two numbers
  - put a counter on that answer on your wing of the ladybird.
- If the answer is already covered on your wing, miss that go.
- The winner is the first player to cover all 6 of the numbers on their wing.

Q3 Write the missing numbers.

6 – ☐ = 5   3 – ☐ = 0   ☐ – 4 = 3

☐ – 0 = 4   9 – ☐ = 4   8 – ☐ = 4

☐ – 6 = 2   ☐ – 3 = 2   ☐ – 4 = 6

9 – ☐ = 5   ☐ – 6 = 1   5 – ☐ = 4

5 – ☐ = 3   4 – ☐ = 2   ☐ – 7 = 2

☐ – 6 = 4   ☐ – 3 = 3   4 – ☐ = 0

7 – ☐ = 2   8 – ☐ = 6   ☐ – 5 = 1

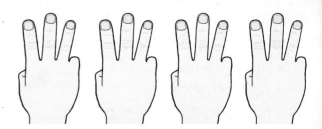

We can think of multiplication as counting on in equal groups. This is called **repeated addition**.

Example

$3 + 3 + 3 + 3 = 12$

$4 \times 3 = 12$

Q1 Write an addition and a multiplication number sentence for each picture.

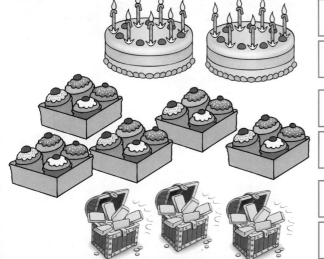

We can also think of multiplication as a picture. This is called an **array**.

$4 \times 3 = 12$ gives the same answer as $3 \times 4 = 12$.

Example

$3 \times 4 = 12$

$4 \times 3 = 12$

Q2 Write **two** multiplication number sentences for each array.

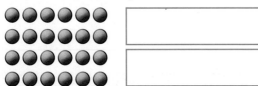

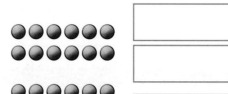

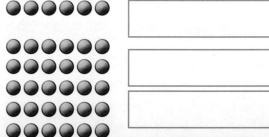

Game: Double the cards

You need: pack of playing cards with the Jacks, Queens and Kings removed and some counters

- Shuffle the cards and place them face down in a pile.
- Take turns to turn over the top card and double the number.
- Cover the answer on the grid with a counter.
- The winner is the first player to complete a line of 4 counters. A line can go sideways, up or down, or diagonally.

4	20	14	8	6
14	10	18	2	6
16	2	10	12	20
8	12	4	14	16
6	10	8	18	12

Q3 Continue each pattern.

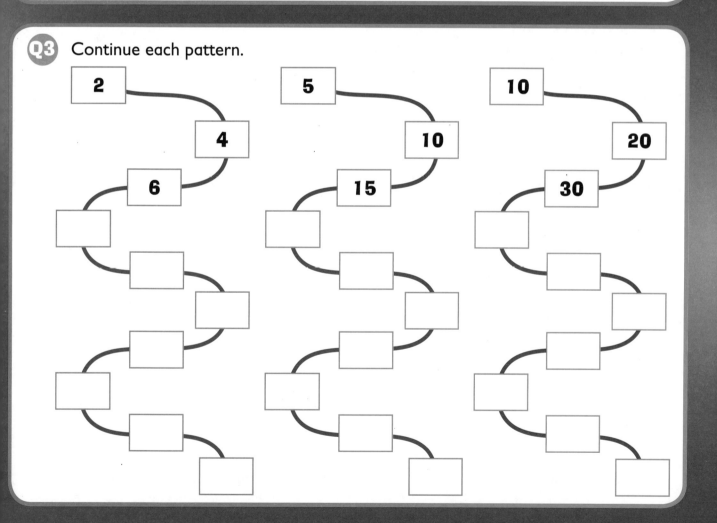

2 — 4 — 6 — □ — □ — □ — □ — □

5 — 10 — 15 — □ — □ — □ — □ — □

10 — 20 — 30 — □ — □ — □ — □ — □

It is important that your child is able to confidently count on and back in steps of 2, 5 and 10. This will help them with recalling the 2, 5 and 10 times tables facts.

Division 1

We can think of division as **sharing**.

Example
Share 12 sweets between 3 children.

$12 \div 3 = 4$

Q1 Share these sweets. Then write the answer to the division number sentence.

Share 6 sweets
between 2 children.

$6 \div 2 = \boxed{}$

Share 8 sweets
between 4 children.

$8 \div 4 = \boxed{}$

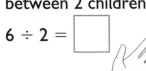

Share 15 sweets
between 5 children.

$15 \div 5 = \boxed{}$

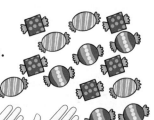

Share 9 sweets
between 3 children.

$9 \div 3 = \boxed{}$

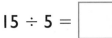
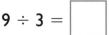

We can also think of division as **grouping**.

Example
How many groups of 2 in 10?

$10 \div 2 = 5$

Q2 Group these pencils. Then write the answer to the division number sentence.

How many groups of 3 in 6?

$6 \div 3 = \boxed{}$

How many groups of 4 in 16?

$16 \div 4 = \boxed{}$

How many groups of 6 in 12?

$12 \div 6 = \boxed{}$

How many groups of 5 in 20?

$20 \div 5 = \boxed{}$

Game: Halve the numbers

You need: paperclip, pencil and some counters

- Before you start, decide who will have the red number cards and who will have the blue number cards.
- Take turns to:
  - spin the spinner
  - halve the number
  - cover the answer on your set of cards with a counter.
- If the answer is already covered on your cards, miss that turn.
- The winner is the first player to cover 6 of their numbers.

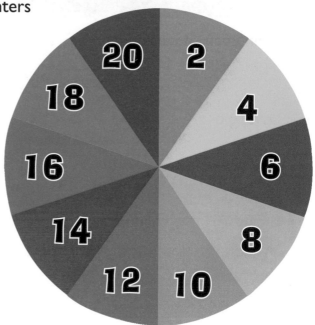

| 1 | 2 | 3 | 4 | 5 | 6 | 7 | 8 | 9 | 10 |

| 1 | 2 | 3 | 4 | 5 | 6 | 7 | 8 | 9 | 10 |

Q3 Answer these.

$8 \div 2 = \boxed{}$ $12 \div 2 = \boxed{}$ Half of $20 = \boxed{}$

$\frac{1}{2}$ of $14 = \boxed{}$ Half of $16 = \boxed{}$ $4 \div 2 = \boxed{}$

$\frac{1}{2}$ of $6 = \boxed{}$ $\frac{1}{2} \times 18 = \boxed{}$ $10 \div 2 = \boxed{}$

There are two ways of looking at division: sharing and grouping. 'Sharing' refers to when a given amount is shared out equally into a given number of sets. 'Grouping' arises from situations where the overall amount and size of each group are known.

Q1 Join each shape to its name.

triangle

 cone

sphere

 cylinder

cuboid

rectangle

circle

square

cube

Q2 What time does each clock show?

Draw hands on each clock to show the time.

1 o'clock

Half past 9

11 o'clock

Q3 What is the weight showing on each of the scales?

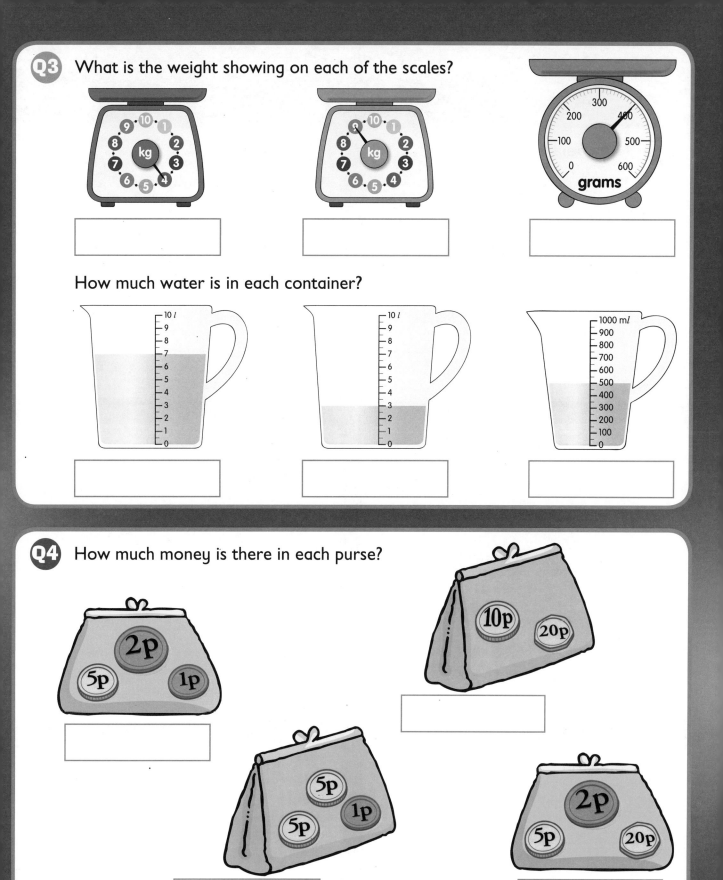

How much water is in each container?

Q4 How much money is there in each purse?

Your child needs to be able to recognise and name a range of 2-D and 3-D shapes of different sizes and in different orientations. They also need to be able to estimate, compare and measure lengths, weights and capacities, and read the numbered divisions on a scale.

Quick Check 1

Q1 Numbers

Continue the pattern.

16, 17, 18, ☐ , ☐ , ☐ , ☐

Order the numbers, smallest first.

26   7   18   15   9

☐ ☐ ☐ ☐ ☐

Fill in the missing numbers.

$28 = $ ☐ $+ 8$ $45 = 40 + $ ☐

Q2 Addition

Write the missing numbers.

$4 + 3 = $ ☐ $8 + 2 = $ ☐

$5 + 1 = $ ☐ $3 + 5 = $ ☐

$7 + $ ☐ $= 10$ ☐ $+ 2 = 9$

$6 + 2 + 1 = $ ☐ $3 + 3 + 5 = $ ☐

Q3 Subtraction

Write the missing numbers.

$8 - 5 = $ ☐ $5 - 1 = $ ☐

$4 - 2 = $ ☐ $9 - 4 = $ ☐

$6 - 5 = $ ☐ $8 - 2 = $ ☐

$3 - $ ☐ $= 0$ $7 - $ ☐ $= 2$

☐ $- 3 = 6$ $10 - $ ☐ $= 5$

Q4 Multiplication

Write the missing numbers.

$4 \times 3 = $ ☐ $5 \times 4 = $ ☐

$3 \times 5 = $ ☐ $2 \times 3 = $ ☐

$4 \times 4 = $ ☐ $5 \times 1 = $ ☐

Double 5 = ☐   Double 7 = ☐

$10 \times 2 = $ ☐ $8 \times 2 = $ ☐

Q5 Division

Write the missing numbers.

$8 \div 2 = $ ☐ $12 \div 4 = $ ☐

$15 \div 5 = $ ☐ $6 \div 3 = $ ☐

$10 \div 2 = $ ☐ $10 \div 5 = $ ☐

$9 \div 3 = $ ☐ $12 \div 6 = $ ☐

$\frac{1}{2}$ of 8 = ☐   Half of 20 = ☐

Q6 Shape, space and measures

Name the shape.

☐

Which is lighter

a or **b**

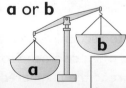

☐

What is the time?

☐

How much money?

☐

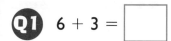

Time how long it takes you to answer the following questions

Q1 6 + 3 = ☐

Q2 Order the numbers, smallest first.

16   54   7   21   36

☐ ☐ ☐ ☐ ☐

Q3 3 + ☐ = 10

Q4 What is the value of the 4 in 47?

☐

Q5 8 − 3 = ☐

Q6 Continue the pattern.

14, 15, 16, 17, ☐ , ☐ , ☐

Q7 20 ÷ 5 = ☐

Q8 Which is more, 41 or 14? ☐

Q9 Double 8 is ☐

Q10 Circle the name of the shape.

square   cylinder

cone   triangle

Q11 4 + 2 = ☐

Q12 What is the time?

☐

Q13 7 − 5 = ☐

Q14 4 + 2 + 5 = ☐

Q15 What is the weight?

☐

Q16 Double 9 = ☐

Q17 12 ÷ 2 = ☐

Q18 How much money?

☐

Q19 Half of 14 is ☐

Q20 8 − ☐ = 6

Score	Time

Numbers 2

Q1 Use the < or > sign to complete these statements.

| 18 | ___ | 30 | | 54 | ___ | 36 | | 72 | ___ | 85 |

| 62 | ___ | 49 | | 37 | ___ | 98 | | 41 | ___ | 14 |

Look at all the numbers in the blue boxes. Write these numbers in order, smallest first.

☐ ☐ ☐ ☐ ☐ ☐

Look at all the numbers in the red boxes. Write these numbers in order, smallest first.

☐ ☐ ☐ ☐ ☐ ☐

Q2 Complete the diagrams.

44
− 10

− 1 **54** + 1

+ 10

− 10

− 1 **81** + 1

+ 10

− 10

− 1 **37** + 1

+ 10

− 10

− 1 **29** + 1

+ 10

Game: And the winner is ...

- For each game:
  - decide who will start with the circle number
  - take turns to count in the steps shown
- The winner is the player who says the star number.

Variation

- Choose different starting numbers, steps and winning numbers.

Game 1 (**2**) on in steps of 1   **15**

Game 2 (**4**) on in steps of 2   **20**

Game 3 (**0**) on in steps of 5   **30**

Game 4 (**10**) on in steps of 10   **80**

Game 5 (**20**) back in steps of 1   **12**

Game 6 (**18**) back in steps of 2   **4**

Game 7 (**50**) back in steps of 5   **10**

Game 8 (**100**) back in steps of 10   **10**

Q3 What is the value of the red digit in each of these numbers?

67 [ ]   42 [ ]   71 [ ]

83 [ ]   59 [ ]   14 [ ]

38 [ ]   96 [ ]   25 [ ]

Q4 Complete each number sentence.

53 = 50 + [ ]   87 = [ ] + 7   29 = 20 + [ ]

32 = [ ] + 2   95 = 90 + [ ]   78 = [ ] + 8

16 = [ ] + 6   64 = 60 + [ ]   41 = [ ] + 1

Your child needs to be able to count on and back in steps of 1, 2, 5 and 10 and recall quickly which number is 1 and 10 more or less than a given number to 100.

Addition 2

Q1 Fill in the missing numbers.

$9 + 3 = \boxed{}$ $4 + 7 = \boxed{}$ $7 + 6 = \boxed{}$

$6 + 5 = \boxed{}$ $9 + 4 = \boxed{}$ $5 + 8 = \boxed{}$

$10 + 6 = \boxed{}$ $4 + 12 = \boxed{}$ $8 + 7 = \boxed{}$

$8 + 4 = \boxed{}$ $6 + 9 = \boxed{}$ $9 + 5 = \boxed{}$

$9 + \boxed{} = 17$ $5 + \boxed{} = 12$ $\boxed{} + 8 = 16$

$\boxed{} + 6 = 20$ $8 + \boxed{} = 11$ $\boxed{} + 13 = 19$

Q2 Complete the diagrams.

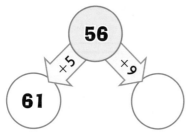
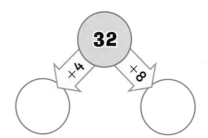

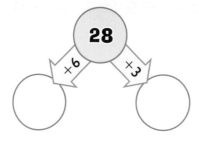
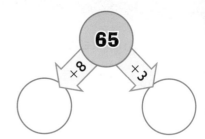

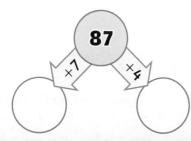
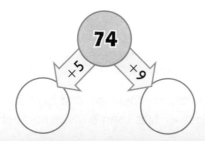

20

Game: Say the total

You need: 12 counters

- Before you start cover each of the numbers with a counter.
- Both players remove a counter and add the two numbers together.
- The first player to call out the correct answer keeps both counters.
- The winner is the player with more counters once all the counters have been removed.

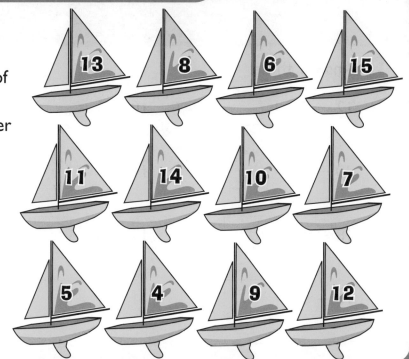

Q3 Add the two balls together.

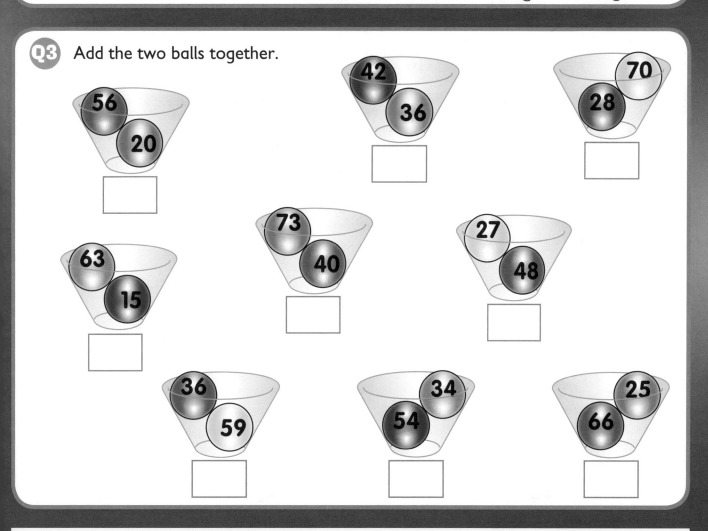

Ensure that your child can recall by heart all the addition number facts to 20. They need to be able to add different combinations of one- and two-digit numbers such as: 37 + 8, 56 + 30 and 42 + 27.

Subtraction 2

Q1 Answer these.

12 − 7 = [ ]　　　10 − 3 = [ ]　　　18 − 9 = [ ]

20 − 15 = [ ]　　　17 − 6 = [ ]　　　14 − 5 = [ ]

18 − 4 = [ ]　　　13 − 8 = [ ]　　　19 − 12 = [ ]

16 − 6 = [ ]　　　11 − 3 = [ ]　　　15 − 14 = [ ]

13 − 11 = [ ]　　　15 − 9 = [ ]　　　16 − 8 = [ ]

14 − 7 = [ ]　　　19 − 15 = [ ]　　　12 − 5 = [ ]

Q2 Complete the diagrams.

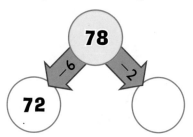

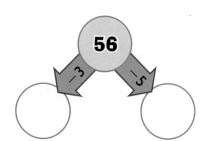

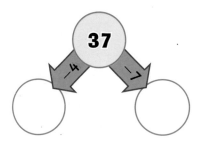

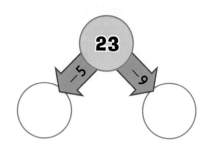

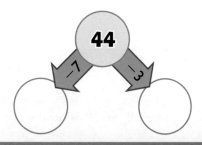

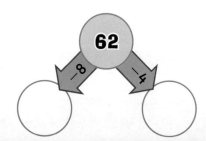

Game: Difference dice

You need: 12 counters

- Before you start cover each of the numbers with a counter.
- Both players remove a counter and find the difference between the two numbers.
- The first player to call out the correct answer keeps both counters.
- The winner is the player with more counters once all the counters have been removed.

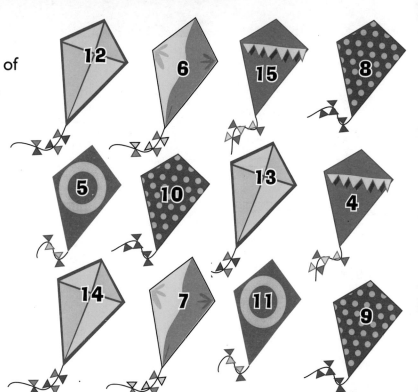

Q3 Find the difference between the two balls.

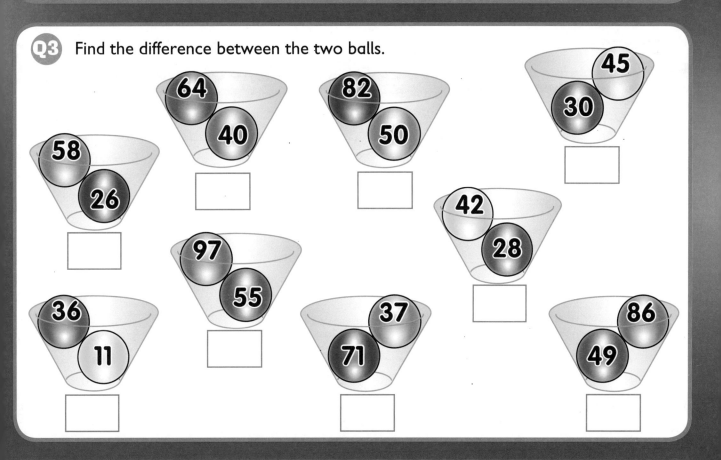

It is important that your child can recall by heart all the subtraction number facts to 20. They need to be able to subtract different combinations of one- and two-digit numbers such as: 43 − 7, 78 − 40 and 65 − 47.

Multiplication 2

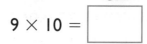
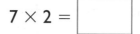

Q1 Answer these.

$2 \times 2 =$ ☐	$4 \times 2 =$ ☐	$9 \times 10 =$ ☐
$7 \times 5 =$ ☐	$6 \times 5 =$ ☐	$7 \times 2 =$ ☐
$9 \times 2 =$ ☐	$3 \times 10 =$ ☐	$10 \times 5 =$ ☐
$3 \times 5 =$ ☐	$8 \times 2 =$ ☐	$4 \times 5 =$ ☐
$8 \times 10 =$ ☐	$9 \times 5 =$ ☐	$6 \times 10 =$ ☐
$6 \times 2 =$ ☐	$7 \times 10 =$ ☐	$8 \times 5 =$ ☐
$4 \times 10 =$ ☐	$2 \times 5 =$ ☐	$3 \times 2 =$ ☐
$10 \times 10 =$ ☐	$5 \times 10 =$ ☐	$5 \times 2 =$ ☐
$5 \times 5 =$ ☐	$10 \times 2 =$ ☐	$2 \times 10 =$ ☐

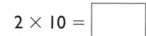

Q2 Write the missing numbers.

☐ $\times 5 = 30$	☐ $\times 10 = 70$	☐ $\times 5 = 20$
☐ $\times 5 = 40$	☐ $\times 10 = 40$	☐ $\times 10 = 50$
☐ $\times 5 = 15$	☐ $\times 5 = 45$	☐ $\times 2 = 12$
☐ $\times 10 = 100$	☐ $\times 2 = 10$	☐ $\times 10 = 30$
☐ $\times 5 = 10$	☐ $\times 2 = 16$	☐ $\times 5 = 50$
☐ $\times 2 = 14$	☐ $\times 2 = 4$	☐ $\times 10 = 60$
☐ $\times 2 = 6$	☐ $\times 5 = 35$	☐ $\times 2 = 8$
☐ $\times 2 = 18$	☐ $\times 2 = 20$	☐ $\times 5 = 25$
☐ $\times 10 = 20$	☐ $\times 10 = 80$	☐ $\times 10 = 90$

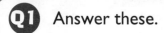
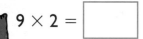

24

Game: 2, 5 or 10 tables

You need: pack of playing cards with the Jacks, Queens and Kings removed

- Before your start:
  – decide if you want to practice the 2, 5 or 10 times table;
  – shuffle the cards and place them face down in a pile.
- Take turns to pick the top card. Both players multiply the card number by the times table you are practising.
- The first player to call out the correct answer keeps the card.
- Continue to take turns to pick a card and each player work out the times table fact.
- When all the cards have been used, the winner is the player with more cards.
- Play the game again, this time practising a different times table.

Q3 Write the numbers that come out of the machines.

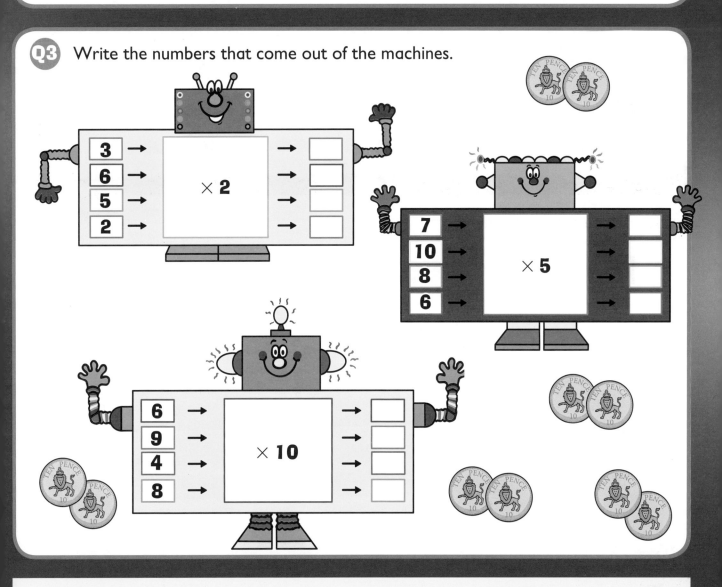

Your child needs to be able to recall instantly the answers to the 2, 5 and 10 times tables. Quick recall of these facts will help your child to learn the answers to other times tables facts up to 10 × 10.

Division 2

Q1 Answer these.

$90 \div 10 =$ ☐ $20 \div 2 =$ ☐ $6 \div 2 =$ ☐

$10 \div 2 =$ ☐ $50 \div 5 =$ ☐ $25 \div 5 =$ ☐

$40 \div 5 =$ ☐ $12 \div 2 =$ ☐ $30 \div 10 =$ ☐

$45 \div 5 =$ ☐ $15 \div 5 =$ ☐ $18 \div 2 =$ ☐

$60 \div 10 =$ ☐ $80 \div 10 =$ ☐ $10 \div 5 =$ ☐

$35 \div 5 =$ ☐ $4 \div 2 =$ ☐ $70 \div 10 =$ ☐

$8 \div 2 =$ ☐ $40 \div 10 =$ ☐ $20 \div 5 =$ ☐

$16 \div 2 =$ ☐ $100 \div 10 =$ ☐ $50 \div 10 =$ ☐

$20 \div 10 =$ ☐ $30 \div 5 =$ ☐ $14 \div 2 =$ ☐

Q2 Write the missing numbers.

☐ $\div 2 = 3$ ☐ $\div 2 = 7$ $4 \div$ ☐ $= 2$

$40 \div$ ☐ $= 4$ $50 \div$ ☐ $= 10$ ☐ $\div 10 = 5$

$10 \div$ ☐ $= 5$ ☐ $\div 5 = 5$ $45 \div$ ☐ $= 9$

☐ $\div 10 = 10$ $90 \div$ ☐ $= 9$ $30 \div$ ☐ $= 3$

$30 \div$ ☐ $= 6$ ☐ $\div 10 = 6$ ☐ $\div 2 = 10$

$18 \div$ ☐ $= 9$ $8 \div$ ☐ $= 4$ $12 \div$ ☐ $= 6$

☐ $\div 5 = 2$ $15 \div$ ☐ $= 3$ ☐ $\div 10 = 8$

$40 \div$ ☐ $= 8$ ☐ $\div 10 = 2$ ☐ $\div 5 = 7$

$70 \div$ ☐ $= 7$ ☐ $\div 2 = 8$ $20 \div$ ☐ $= 4$

Game: Dividing by 2, 5 or 10

- Take turns to choose a number from below.
- If you choose a number in a ⭐, ask your partner to divide that number by 2.
- If you choose a number in a ☁, ask your partner to divide that number by 5.
- If you choose a red number, ask your partner to divide that number by 10.
- If you choose a number such a 20, you can ask your partner to divide that number by 2, 5 or 10!

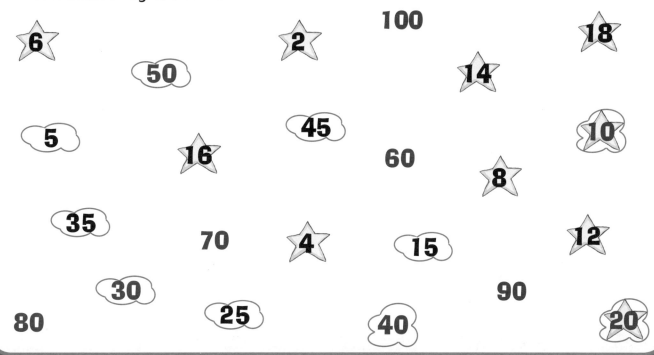

Q3 Divide the numbers hit by an arrow. Write the answer in the same coloured box as the arrow.

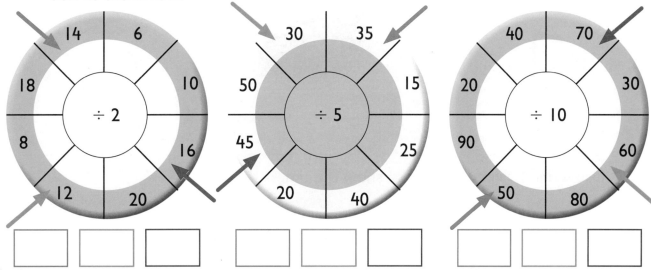

Encouraging your child to see the link between a times table fact and the related division fact, i.e. 6 × 5 = 30 and 30 ÷ 5 = 6, will help your child to remember both facts more quickly.

Q1 Join each shape to its name. Then inside the shape write the number of sides (2-D) or faces (3-D) the shape has. One has been done for you.

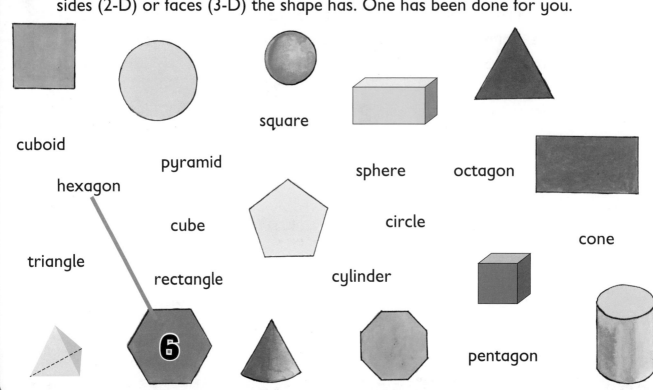

cuboid

square

pyramid

sphere

octagon

hexagon

cube

circle

cone

triangle

rectangle

cylinder

6

pentagon

Q2 What time does each clock show?

Draw hands on each clock to show the time.

Half past 5

Quarter to 3

Quarter past 9

Q3 Draw an arrow on each set of scales to show the weight on the label.

5 kg

$8\frac{1}{2}$ kg

200 g

Colour each container to show the amount of water on the label.

8 l

$6\frac{1}{2}$ l

300 ml

Q4 On the label write how much money there is in the purse. Then work out how much change you would get from the coin shown on the hand.

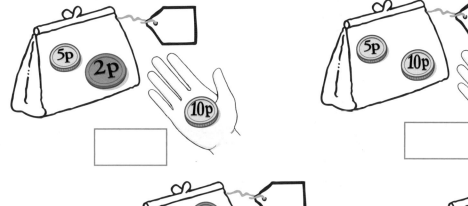

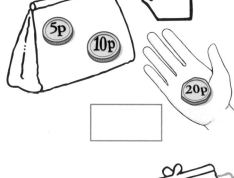

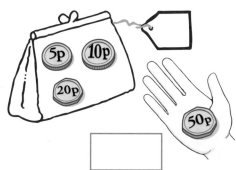

Ensure that your child is able to tell and write quarter past and quarter to times for Q2. They also need to find totals and give change for Q4.

Quick Check 2

Q1 Numbers

Make each statement true by using < or >.

16 ☐ 68   44 ☐ 29

Order the numbers, smallest first.

84   50   62   29   58

☐ ☐ ☐ ☐ ☐

What is the value of each red digit?

72 ☐   48 ☐   35 ☐

Q2 Addition

Write the missing numbers.

$7 + 8 =$ ☐ $9 + 5 =$ ☐

$6 +$ ☐ $= 19$ ☐ $+ 3 = 16$

$45 + 3 =$ ☐ $73 + 8 =$ ☐

$53 + 30 =$ ☐ $46 + 23 =$ ☐

Q3 Subtraction

Write the missing numbers.

$15 - 7 =$ ☐ $11 - 9 =$ ☐

$19 -$ ☐ $= 5$ ☐ $- 8 = 6$

$58 - 6 =$ ☐ $81 - 5 =$ ☐

$94 - 50 =$ ☐ $42 - 30 =$ ☐

$68 - 45 =$ ☐ $73 - 56 =$ ☐

Q4 Multiplication

Write the missing numbers.

$6 \times 2 =$ ☐ $3 \times 10 =$ ☐

$7 \times 5 =$ ☐ $9 \times 2 =$ ☐

$4 \times 10 =$ ☐ $8 \times 5 =$ ☐

$5 \times 5 =$ ☐ $6 \times 10 =$ ☐

$4 \times 2 =$ ☐ $9 \times 5 =$ ☐

Q5 Division

Write the missing numbers.

$14 \div 2 =$ ☐ $15 \div 5 =$ ☐

$50 \div 10 =$ ☐ $20 \div 2 =$ ☐

$30 \div 5 =$ ☐ $80 \div 10 =$ ☐

$16 \div 2 =$ ☐ $100 \div 10 =$ ☐

$20 \div 5 =$ ☐ $10 \div 2 =$ ☐

Q6 Shape, space and measures

How many faces on a cuboid?

☐

Show $\frac{1}{4}$ past 8

Show $3\frac{1}{2}$ kg

How much change from 20p?

☐

Time Test 2

Q1 $14 + 5 =$ ☐

Q2 True or false?

$56 > 67$ ☐

Q3 $3 +$ ☐ $= 10$

Q4 $87 =$ ☐ $+ 7$

Q5 $13 - 7 =$ ☐

Q6
10 less		10 more
☐	52	☐

Q7 $35 \div 5 =$ ☐

Q8 $56 + 40 =$ ☐

Q9 $6 \times 10 =$ ☐

Q10 What is the time?

☐

Q11 $72 + 9 =$ ☐

Q12 How much money?

☐

Q13 $41 - 6 =$ ☐

Q14 $7 \times 5 =$ ☐

Q15 Show $9\frac{1}{2}$ litres.

Q16 $57 + 28 =$ ☐

Q17 $30 \div 10 =$ ☐

Q18 $82 - 54 =$ ☐

Q19 $9 \times 2 =$ ☐

Q20 How much change from 20p?

☐

Score	Time

31

Answers

Numbers 1
Page 4

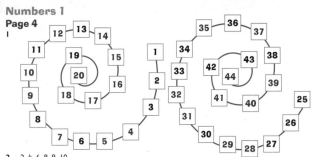

2 2, 4, 6, 8, 9, 10
1, 5, 7, 11, 12, 17
3, 18, 25, 30, 36, 41
3, 4, 7, 9, 17, 30

Page 5
3

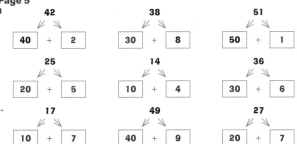

Other answers are possible.

Addition 2
Page 6
1
$3 + 1 = 4$	$6 + 2 = 8$	$10 + 0 = 10$
$2 + 5 = 7$	$3 + 3 = 6$	$4 + 4 = 8$
$5 + 5 = 10$	$4 + 2 = 6$	$6 + 3 = 9$
$7 + 2 = 9$	$9 + 1 = 10$	$2 + 8 = 10$
$4 + 3 = 7$	$2 + 2 = 4$	$3 + 5 = 8$
$8 + 1 = 9$	$5 + 4 = 9$	$2 + 3 = 5$

2
$2 + 3 + 1 = 6$	$2 + 4 + 3 = 9$	$3 + 4 + 2 = 9$
$4 + 2 + 2 = 8$	$5 + 1 + 2 = 8$	$2 + 1 + 7 = 10$
$1 + 2 + 5 = 8$	$2 + 2 + 3 + 4 = 11$	$6 + 2 + 3 = 11$
$4 + 1 + 5 = 10$	$3 + 2 + 1 + 1 = 7$	$5 + 3 + 4 = 12$

Page 7
3 Answers for 10 may include:
0 + 10   1 + 9   2 + 8
4 + 6   5 + 5

Answers for 20 may include:
0 + 20   1 + 19   2 + 18
3 + 17   5 + 15   6 + 14
7 + 13   8 + 12   9 + 11
10 + 10

Subtraction 1
Page 8
1
$3 - 1 = 2$	$6 - 2 = 4$	$4 - 3 = 1$
$7 - 2 = 5$	$5 - 2 = 3$	$2 - 2 = 0$
$8 - 5 = 3$	$10 - 8 = 2$	$6 - 3 = 3$
$7 - 4 = 3$	$9 - 3 = 6$	$5 - 4 = 1$

2
$5 - 3 = 2$	$4 - 1 = 3$	$7 - 3 = 4$
$10 - 5 = 5$	$6 - 4 = 2$	$8 - 7 = 1$
$9 - 6 = 3$	$3 - 2 = 1$	$10 - 7 = 3$
$8 - 3 = 5$	$4 - 2 = 2$	$9 - 2 = 7$

Page 9
3
$6 - 1 = 5$	$3 - 3 = 0$	$7 - 4 = 3$
$4 - 0 = 4$	$9 - 5 = 4$	$8 - 4 = 4$
$8 - 6 = 2$	$5 - 3 = 2$	$10 - 4 = 6$
$9 - 4 = 5$	$7 - 6 = 1$	$5 - 1 = 4$
$5 - 2 = 3$	$4 - 2 = 2$	$9 - 7 = 2$
$10 - 6 = 4$	$6 - 3 = 3$	$4 - 4 = 0$
$7 - 5 = 2$	$8 - 2 = 6$	$6 - 5 = 1$

Multiplication 1
Page 10
1
$7 + 7 = 14$	$4 + 4 + 4 + 4 + 4 = 20$	$6 + 6 + 6 = 18$
$2 \times 7 = 14$	$5 \times 4 = 20$	$3 \times 6 = 18$

2
$6 \times 4 = 24$	$2 \times 6 = 12$
$4 \times 6 = 24$	$6 \times 2 = 12$
$5 \times 3 = 15$	$6 \times 5 = 30$
$3 \times 5 = 15$	$5 \times 6 = 30$

Page 11
3

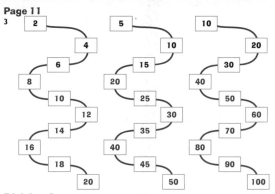

Division 1
Page 12
1
$6 \div 2 = 3$	$8 \div 4 = 2$	
$15 \div 5 = 3$	$9 \div 3 = 3$	

2
$6 \div 3 = 2$	$16 \div 4 = 4$
$12 \div 6 = 2$	$20 \div 5 = 4$

Page 13
3
$8 \div 2 = 4$	$12 \div 2 = 6$	Half of $20 = 10$
½ of $14 = 7$	Half of $16 = 8$	$4 \div 2 = 2$
½ of $6 = 3$	½ × $18 = 9$	$10 \div 2 = 5$

Shape, space and measures 1
Page 14
1

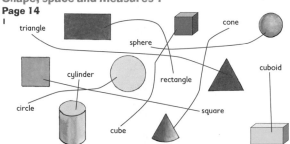

triangle   cone   sphere   rectangle   cuboid   cylinder   circle   square   cube

2 half past 4   7 o'clock   half past 2

Page 15
3
4 kg	9 kg	400 g
7 l	3 l	500 ml

4
8p	30p
11p	27p

Quick Check 1
Page 16

Q1 Numbers
16, 17, 18, 19, 20, 21, 22

7, 9, 15, 18, 26

$28 = 20 + 8$ $45 = 40 + 5$

Q2 Addition
$4 + 3 = 7$	$8 + 2 = 10$
$5 + 1 = 6$	$3 + 5 = 8$
$7 + 3 = 10$	$7 + 2 = 9$
$6 + 2 + 1 = 9$	$3 + 3 + 5 = 11$

Q3 Subtraction
$8 - 5 = 3$	$5 - 1 = 4$
$4 - 2 = 2$	$9 - 4 = 5$
$6 - 5 = 1$	$8 - 2 = 6$
$3 - 3 = 0$	$7 - 5 = 2$
$9 - 3 = 6$	$10 - 5 = 5$

Q4 Multiplication
$4 \times 3 = 12$	$5 \times 4 = 20$
$3 \times 5 = 15$	$2 \times 3 = 6$
$4 \times 4 = 16$	$5 \times 1 = 5$
Double 5 = 10	Double 7 = 14
$10 \times 2 = 20$	$8 \times 2 = 16$

Q5 Division
$8 \div 2 = 4$	$12 \div 4 = 3$
$15 \div 5 = 3$	$6 \div 3 = 2$
$10 \div 2 = 5$	$10 \div 5 = 2$
$9 \div 3 = 3$	$12 \div 6 = 2$
½ of $8 = 4$	Half of $20 = 10$

Q6 Shape, space and measures
cube	half past 7
b	22p

Time Test 1
Page 17
1 $6 + 3 = 9$	8 41	15 7 kg
2 7, 16, 21, 36, 54	9 16	16 18
3 $3 + 7 = 10$	10 cylinder	17 $12 \div 2 = 6$
4 40	11 $4 + 2 = 6$	18 17p
5 $8 - 3 = 5$	12 2 o'clock	19 7
6 14, 15, 16, 17, 18, 19, 20	13 $7 - 5 = 2$	20 $8 - 2 = 6$
7 $20 \div 5 = 4$	14 $4 + 2 + 5 = 11$	